Simply Cursive – Style #1

By: Sheri Graham

Published in the United States of America by:
Graham Family Ministries
P. O. Box 826
Moundridge, KS 67107

Our Website: www.SheriGraham.com
Email: sheri@sherigraham.com

Includes artwork by Trina of www.digiscrapkits.com.

All Scripture references are from the KJV.

Introduction

Welcome to **Simply Cursive – Style #1**! After the release of my *Create Your Own Penmanship Pages* series, I had so many contact me asking for a cursive book. I listened and now have completed the first in this series.

This book is divided up into two main sections: the **Cursive Lessons** and the **Extra Practice Pages**.

The Cursive Lessons have been grouped together so that your child will learn similar style letters one right after the other. After every five or so lessons is a Review lesson to reinforce what has been learned so far.

Each lesson has a couple lines for your child to trace the letters, then additional lines to copy and write the letters on their own. I also used the font with arrows so your child can easily see how to write each letter in cursive.

You can do one lesson a day or divide it up over two days. It really depends on the age of your child and their readiness to learn cursive. As the parent, you decide what is best for your child!

The Extra Practice Pages include selected Bible passages for your child to copy in cursive. These pages can be used however you feel is most helpful, having your child write out the whole passage in one sitting or dividing it up over several days.

I have also included a few lessons to practice writing numbers. Since some choose to teach their children cursive before printing, I decided to include some numbers practice as well.

How to use this book: As stated above, you can do one lesson a day or divide it up and do one lesson over two days. If you do one lesson a day plus use some of the Extra Practice Pages, your child can work through this book in one semester. If you decide to take things a bit slower and do one lesson over two days plus some of the Extra Practice Pages, your child will take close to the whole year to complete it.

You may wonder how I came up with my title for this series: "**Simply Cursive**"...well, I think as with many things we teach our children, we make things too complicated and complex. I wanted to provide a cursive book that would be simple to use and reasonably priced. I hope you and your children enjoy it!

In Christ,
Sheri

Cursive Handwriting Guide - Style #1

A a   B b   C c

D d   E e   F f

G g   H h   I i   J j

K k   L l   M m   N n

O o   P p   Q q

R r   S s   T t   U u

V v   W w   X x

Y y   Z z

0 1 2 3 4 5 6 7 8 9

Proper Hand & Paper Position

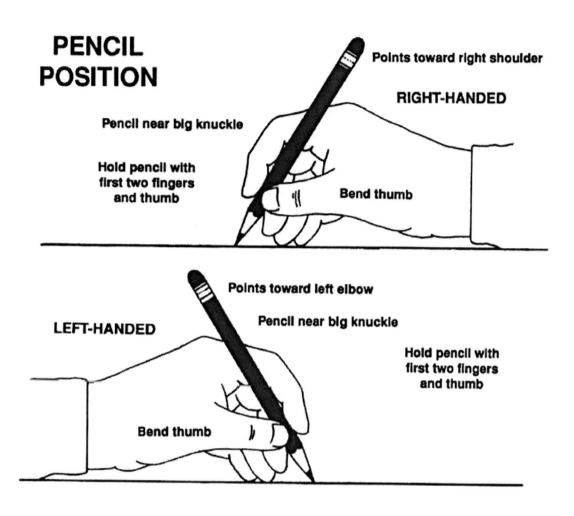

PENCIL POSITION

Points toward right shoulder

RIGHT-HANDED

Pencil near big knuckle

Hold pencil with first two fingers and thumb

Bend thumb

Points toward left elbow

Pencil near big knuckle

LEFT-HANDED

Hold pencil with first two fingers and thumb

Bend thumb

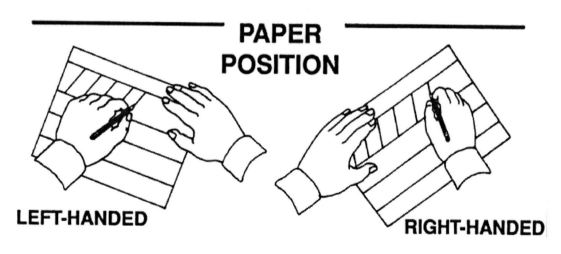

PAPER POSITION

LEFT-HANDED

RIGHT-HANDED

Cursive Lessons

Lowercase Letters

Under Curves

Lesson 1 – l ℓ

ℓ ℓ ℓ ℓ ℓ ℓ

ℓ ℓ ℓ ℓ ℓ ℓ

ℓ ℓ ℓ

ℓ ℓ ℓ

ℓ ℓ ℓ

ℓ

ℓ

ℓ

ℓ

Lesson 2 – i i

Lesson 3 – † t

t t t t t t

t t t t t t

t t t

t t t

t t t

t

t

t

t

Lesson 4 – e *e*

e e e e e e

e e e e e e

e e e

e e e

e e e

e

e

e

e

Lesson 5 – h *h*

h   h   h   h   h   h

h   h   h   h   h   h

h   h   h

h   h   h

h   h   h

h

h

h

h

Lesson 6 - Review

l

i

t

e

h

li   *le*

ti   *te*

hi   *he*

it   *ill*

Lesson 7 – r ɾ

Lesson 8 – S $\mathscr{s}$

Lesson 9 – b ℓ

Lesson 10 – j j

Lesson 11 – u _u_

Lesson 12 - Review

r

s

b

j

it

ru   su

bu   ju

he   jet

rub   sit

Lesson 13 – k k

Lesson 14 – p _p_

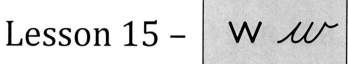

Lesson 16 – f f

Lesson 17 - Review

_k_

_p_

_w_

_f_

will   kit

pet   file

bell   pup

wise   kite

see   the

Lowercase Letters Over Curves

Lesson 18 – n n

n n n n n n

n n n n n n

n n n

n n n

n n n

n

n

n

n

Lesson 19 – m m

Lesson 20 – Y y

Lesson 21 – ∨ ⱱ

Lesson 22 – Z z

Lesson 23 – $\times$ x

Lesson 24 - Review

$\mathscr{N}$

$\mathscr{M}$

$\mathscr{Y}$

$\mathscr{V}$

$\mathscr{J}$

$\mathscr{X}$

men   vet

key   him

sew   hill

Lowercase
Letters
Down Curves

Lesson 25 – a a

a a a a a a

a a a a a a

a a a

a a a

a a a

a

a

a

a

Lesson 26 – C C

𝒞   𝒞   𝒞   𝒞   𝒞   𝒞   𝒞

𝒞   𝒞   𝒞   𝒞   𝒞   𝒞   𝒞

𝒞   𝒞   𝒞

𝒞   𝒞   𝒞

𝒞   𝒞   𝒞

𝒞

𝒞

𝒞

𝒞

Lesson 27 – g g

g g g g g g

g g g g g g

g g g

g g g

g g g

g

g

g

g

Lesson 28 – d d

d d d d d d

d d d d d d

d d d

d d d

d d d

d

d

d

d

Lesson 29 – o o

Lesson 30 – q q

q q q q q q

q q q q q q

q q q

q q q

q q q

q

q

q

q

Lesson 31 - Review

a

c

g

d

o

q

dog   cat

bag   hot

peg   lad

"*Hook*"

Connections

Lesson 32 – *br*

br br br br br

br br br br br

br   br   br

br   br   br

br   br   br

br

br

br

brag

Lesson 33 – be

be   be   be   be   be

be   be   be   be   be

be   be   be

be   be   be

be   be   be

be

be

be

bell

Lesson 34 – *or*

or   or   or   or   or

or   or   or   or   or

or   or   or

or   or   or

or   or   or

or

or

or

for

Lesson 35 – *os*

os   os   os   os   os

os   os   os   os   os

os   os   os

os   os   os

os   os   os

os

os

os

cross

Lesson 36 – *ur*

ur   ur   ur   ur   ur

ur   ur   ur   ur   ur

ur   ur   ur

ur   ur   ur

ur   ur   ur

ur

ur

ur

wrong

Uppercase Letters

Lesson 37 – A a

a a a a a

a a a a a

a a a

a a a

a a a

a

a

a

a

Lesson 38 – C C

C   C   C   C   C

C   C   C   C   C

C   C   C

C   C   C

C   C   C

C

C

C

C

Lesson 39 –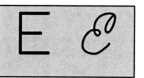

Lesson 40 – N n

Lesson 41 – M m

Lesson 42 - Review

a

c

e

n

m

Alex   Eve

Christ

Noah

Matt

Lesson 43 – U u

Lesson 44 –

Lesson 45 –

Lesson 46 –

Lesson 47 –

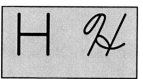

Lesson 48 - Review

U

V

W

Y

H

Under   Vet

Will

Yam

Hellen

Lesson 49 – Z z

Lesson 50 –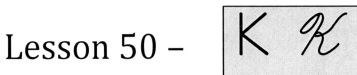

Lesson 51 –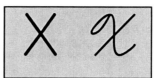

Lesson 52 –

Lesson 53 – B 𝓑

Lesson 54 - Review

Y

K

X

Q

B

Zoo   *Kate*

Xebec

Queen

Bobby

Lesson 55 –

Lesson 56 –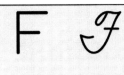

Lesson 57 –

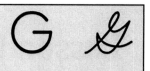

Lesson 58 – $\boxed{I \; \ell}$

Lesson 59 - Review

D

F

G

I

Dad

Frank

Glen

Isaiah

Dan

Lesson 60 – $\mathcal{J}$ $\mathcal{g}$

$\mathcal{G}$ $\mathcal{G}$ $\mathcal{G}$ $\mathcal{G}$ $\mathcal{G}$

$\mathcal{G}$ $\mathcal{G}$ $\mathcal{G}$ $\mathcal{G}$ $\mathcal{G}$

$\mathcal{G}$ $\mathcal{G}$ $\mathcal{G}$

$\mathcal{G}$ $\mathcal{G}$ $\mathcal{G}$

$\mathcal{G}$ $\mathcal{G}$ $\mathcal{G}$

$\mathcal{G}$

$\mathcal{G}$

$\mathcal{G}$

$\mathcal{G}$

Lesson 61 –   L $\mathcal{L}$

Lesson 62 – O O

Lesson 63 - Review

J

L

O

J

L

O

Jesus

Love

Oscar

Lesson 64 –

P $\mathcal{P}$

Lesson 65 – R R

R R R R R

R R R R R

R R R

R R R

R R R

R

R

R

R

Lesson 66 –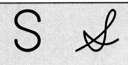

Lesson 67 –

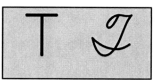

Lesson 68 - Review

P

R

S

T

Peter

Robert

Sarah

Jimmy

Rachel

Lesson 69 - Review

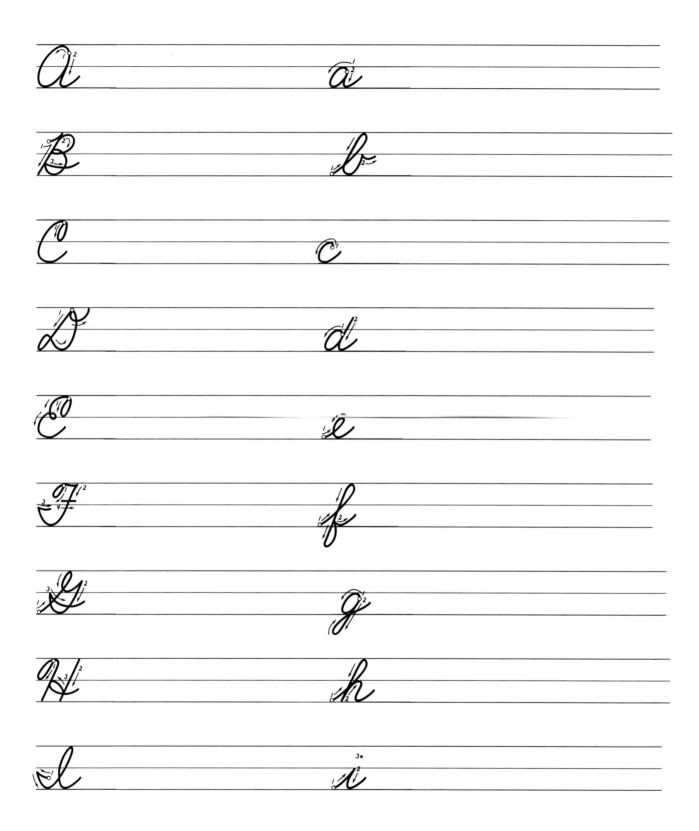

Lesson 70 - Review

Lesson 71 - Review

Lesson 72 - Numbers

1

1

2

2

3

3

4

4

Lesson 73 - Numbers

5

5

6

6

7

7

8

8

Lesson 74 - Numbers

9

9

10

10

1   2

3   4

5   6

7   8

9   10

Extra Practice Pages

Psalm 1:1

Blessed is the man that walketh

not in the counsel of the

ungodly, nor standeth in the

way of sinners, nor sitteth in

the seat of the scornful.

Psalm 1:2

But his delight is in the law of

the Lord; and in his law doth

he meditate day and night.

Psalm 1:3

And he shall be like a tree

planted by the rivers of water,

that bringeth forth his fruit in

his season; his leaf also shall

not wither; and whatsoever he

doeth shall prosper.

Psalm 1:4

The ungodly are not so: but are

like the chaff which the wind

driveth away.

Psalm 1:5

Therefore the ungodly shall not

stand in the judgment, nor

sinners in the congregation of

the righteous.

Psalm 1:6

For the Lord knoweth the way

of the righteous: but the way of

the ungodly shall perish.

Psalm 23

The Lord is my shepherd; I

shall not want.   He maketh

me to lie down in green

pastures: he leadeth me beside

the still waters.   He restoreth

my soul: he leadeth me in the

paths of righteousness for his

name's sake. Yea, though I

walk through the valley of the

shadow of death, I will fear

no evil: for thou art with me;

thy rod and thy staff they

comfort me. Thou preparest a

table before me in the presence

of mine enemies: thou anointest

my head with oil; my cup

runneth over. Surely goodness

and mercy shall follow me all

the days of my life: and I

will dwell in the house of the

Lord for ever.

Matthew 11:28-30

Come unto me, all ye that

labour and are heavy laden,

and I will give you rest.

Take my yoke upon you, and

learn of me; for I am meek

and lowly in heart: and ye

shall find rest unto your souls.

For my yoke is easy, and my

burden is light.

Matthew 6:9-13

After this manner therefore pray

ye. Our Father which art in

heaven, Hallowed be thy name.

Thy kingdom come. Thy will be

done in earth, as it is in

heaven. Give us this day our

daily bread. And forgive us our

debts, as we forgive our

debtors. And lead us not into

temptation, but deliver us from

evil. For thine is the kingdom,

and the power, and the glory,

for ever. Amen.

Sheri Graham is a homeschool mom of 5 blessings. She enjoys being home with her family and using her talents to not only serve her family but to help others in their walks as wives and mothers (and daughters of the King!).

At the heart of Graham Family Ministries is ministering to the Christian family and using the gifts that the Lord has given each of us. Through our website (http://www.SheriGraham.com) we provide articles, downloads, ebooks, and links on homemaking and homeschooling topics, as well as information on other resources that hopefully will encourage you as you grow and learn together as a family. May the Lord bless each of you as you walk with Him each step of the way!

Be sure to subscribe to Sheri's blog to keep updated on new products, receive yummy recipes, and homemaking and homeschooling tips! You will be blessed!

You can find Sheri online at:

www.SheriGraham.com (My main website and blog)
www.SheriGraham.com/IntentionalPlanner (The Intentional Planner Website)
www.12weekholidayplanner.com (The Holiday Planner website)
www.Homeschooling-Central.com (My free homeschooling site!)

CPSIA information can be obtained at www.ICGtesting.com
Printed in the USA
LVOW09s1233300314

379538LV00011B/547/P

9 781496 180162